The Startup Mum

How to grow million dollar businesses & have babies at the same time.

(using the power of the Internet)

By Hermione Way

Featuring 6 other global startup mums.

Dedication

For Venice Vivienne and Octavius Max, sometimes I feel like a bad mother because I work a lot, I should be watching you instead of sending the email on my phone.

But I hope you will read this one day and realise I'm working hard for your future, for you to thrive, money isn't everything but it's a facilitator. I hope the Internet gives you the freedom to change the world for better and make money from wherever, whenever you want.

For my mother Caroline aka Mutti Mama for just about everything, inspiring my creativity, teaching me to take opportunity as it presents itself and also not to take life too seriously. Oh oh and the love, all the unconditional love, kisses & cuddles.

For Serhan, the rather large tree trunk who is the anchor & allows me to be the hurricane ;)

For my big brother Ben for being a genius and trailblazing at such a young age.

For my dad Christopher for teaching my strong work ethic, my love of nature and appreciating the small things in life.

For my younger brothers Theo & Monty for being feminists & environmentalists.

For Simon MacDowall for being my publisher guru.

Synopsis:

From breastfeeding in the boardroom to pumping for pitch time, It's not glamorous, it's not easy, it's not pretty, but through sheer determination, grit and a lot of awkward moments, it can be done. The Startup Mum gives an unprecedented look at these new mums who are breaking down barriers, tearing down stereotypes and shaping the new world of work by building million dollar businesses and having children at the same time. This is a candid book on how, with a lot of help, a vision, and the will to make it happen, women all over the world no longer have to choose between having kids and having a career or having to wait to have kids whilst they build their career first because leveraging the Internet they can do both at the same time.

About the Author:

Hermione Way is an entrepreneur, journalist and communications specialist who has been working in the technology industry for over 10 years. She was the Silicon Valley Video Director for The Next Web and her video blog became a media partner of TechCrunch.
She has founded a number of ventures including Newspepper.com, Techfluff.tv, Ignite Wellness, WayMedia Startup World.info, TechDrive.co, Hollywood Meets Silicon Valley, Startup Stowmarket, Free The Seas.org and The Sustainable Entrepreneur's Club.

She was the main cast member of the show Startups Silicon Valley, a $25million TV show, broadcasting to 88 million homes on the Bravo TV network.

She was the co-founder of the world's first smart vibrator www.vibease.com - achieving over $1.5million in sales and shipping 20,000 devices worldwide.

In 2015, as the former Head Of European Communications at Tinder, Hermione helped grow the brand across the UK, France, Germany, Russia, Spain & Italy. At Tinder she worked on forging first of a kind partnerships with the NHS and a voting engagement initiative for the 2016 EU Referendum.

She is currently Head Of Global Growth at ZoomSphere.com - a social media software company.

She now helps companies become more parent friendly so they don't miss out on talent due to inflexibility in the workplace.

She is a mum of 2 Venice aged 4.5 and Octavius aged 1.5.

tl;dr:

It's fucking hard, get help, a co-founder on the business side and full-time childcare on the family side.

Introduction

The Internet has dawned a new era in how we work and where we work, going are the days of traveling to an office, doing the 9-5 in a corporate office for your entire working life. Humans are not binary creatures, we are creative by our very nature and so boxing us into one space for 40 hours a week does not lead to high levels of productivity or creativity, which is ultimately problem solving.

People need different environments to draw inspiration & spark creativity. The market is also telling us this will be the future way of working with co-working company WeWork being valued at $20billion.

So what does this new change mean for women in the workplace?

It means a lot more freedom and flexibility. There was once (and still is in certain respects) a mantra of women having to choose between having a career and having children, but I believe the Internet gives women a platform to do both at the same time.

There has also been a mantra of women 'having it all" (a career and children) but this has meant children being dropped off at nursery and women commuting to an office and back, often missing out on collecting their kids from school or having dinner with their children.

Or "having it all" has often meant women working on their careers until their mid thirties and then becoming a mother later on if life which can lead to a whole host of other problems with conception and fertility. (Believe me I know having suffered from miscarriages and infertility).

Let's be real.

This book does not aim to glamourise having babies and starting companies at the same time because I don't want readers to get unrealistic expectations, both starting a company and having a child are two incredibly difficult things to do alone, let alone at the same time.

I also don't want to make anyone who chooses not to do either feel ostracised, I respect your choices, there are a million different paths to take.

The goal for this book is to highlight the new feminine power rising, money is power and by showing the world women can attain wealth and power in the way that they want to work, makes the status quo bend to us, it makes the patriarch stand up and listen that there is another way to do business, to gain power. By telling these stories we want to encourage the workplace to bend to us, we want the workplace to suit our needs, we demand change.

Why am I qualified to write this book?

I'm not personally a millionaire... quite yet, but in 2014, whilst I was pregnant and gave birth to my first child, my startup Vibease achieved over $1.5 million in sales, of our smart vibrator. I continued to work throughout pregnancy and post birth between a mixture of taking my baby to work and working from my home office.

How do you define "million dollar companies?"

A million of anything is by no means a small feat, for the purpose of this book it means either over 1 million paying users, valuation of over $1 million, revenue of over $1 million or raising capital of over $1 million.

Where was at I in my career when I decided to have kids?

In 2013 I was at the height of my career as a high profile startup founder in Silicon Valley and I saw no way of have children. Being the founder of a technology startup that was growing fast and getting plenty of media attention, I was on the 'startup high' and could not see where having children could fit into this.

Any entrepreneur knows that you have to be 100% in the game to win. I basically lived on an airplane doing deals all over the world. I was 29-years-old and I knew I definitely did not want to miss out on having kids but I had worked relentlessly for 10 years' to get to this place of relative "success" and was I really going to let it all go, now?

I knew If I kept going I could be more successful, my company would grow bigger. But I also knew that if I didn't change my trajectory fast I would end up super successful but maybe missing out on a big part of my ultimate life goal which was experiencing motherhood.

There is a famous expression in the world of startups that you "jump out of a plane and build your parachute on the way down" - meaning you have to launch a product first and figure out how it's going to make money or how it's going to grow after. I thought, I could do all the planning in the world to have children but if I didn't actually do it it soon it may be a missed opportunity. In the meantime I had met a really great guy who I could see being the father of my children (luckily he agreed).

So I metaphorically jumped out of the plane and got pregnant.

Hardest parts?

The first hardest part was to tell my co-founder that I was pregnant, I waited until quite late, maybe around 6 months as I wanted to make sure my pregnancy was qualified. Luckily my co-founder Dema Tio was extremely supportive and I was keen to tell him I wanted to continue to work throughout pregnancy and after the birth as much as I could.

I continued to pitch for funding whilst pregnant and there was an awkward day when I was pitching Comcast Ventures in San Francisco - I arrived maybe 8 months pregnant and there were five to six 40+ year-old men sitting around the boardroom, remember I was pregnant and pitching the world's first smart clitoral stimulator. Although the men were very friendly, they were clearly embarrassed when I started talking about the health benefits of female orgasm and decided to pass on this investment!

The day after my daughter was born I had a call with an investor over Skype so I just breastfed my baby and continued the call, I was sitting on my couch at home.

When I left Tinder in 2017 I set up a very successful consulting business. My husband at the time was my CFO so he was helping me with the business financials but it was up to me to do sales. I pitched a new client in London and I was completely transparent and upfront with him saying: "i've just had a baby and I'm still breastfeeding so if you'd like to engage me I'm afraid you'll have to be ok with me bringing my baby to the office. He was very positive, sending me pictures of his kid. I bought my newborn baby on the four hour round trip twice before he hired me and then two weeks after he hired me, he called to say he wanted to fire me, to cancel the contract because he had found someone else to do the work. If bringing my newborn baby to work wasn't a sign of commitment I don't know what is. Oh well, you win some, you lose some, I prefer to let it go!

The dark days

There have been a number of extremely dark days, days where you're so tired you don't know how you are going to get through the day, days where you think:"why do people bother having children when it's so bloody difficult?" and "what the hell have I done?". It sounds cliche but every day gets slightly easier and you have to take one day at a time.

Find an amazing co-founder

My co-founder Dema Tio was based in Singapore, he was responsible for manufacturing the product in China and I, global sales and marketing. We worked well as a team from the beginning and he always said: "family first". How did I find him? He found me as he was looking for a female co-founder who was sex positive and he saw me on a TV show called "Startups Silicon Valley" on the Bravo TV network. He wanted me to join for a long time and I was working on other projects, but eventually I was looking for my next thing and it was the right time to work together. Even though I continued to work throughout pregnancy and after birth he really took the responsibility of making sure the product was ready to ship and the company was driving forward at the time when I had just given birth and was not able to be out and about so much.

It gets easier as they grow

Everyone says "it does get easier" and they are right, it does! For maybe the first three years I spent time thinking "why do people have children, where is the joy?" People told me "it gets easier" but I couldn't believe them because it was so hard for so many years, now my daughter is 4 and we've just got out of the terrible twos (yes they lasted until aged 4!) Now they are growing up and can do more for themselves, I want more children!

How have I done it?

With lots of help! Let's be clear; you cannot even write one email with a baby or toddler around pawing at your keypad. You need the hours to work so you must find help.

The way to grow your company is to just keep working relentlessly at it, but that means you need to find the care to look after your children during office hours.

Raising a kid is a full-time job and once I realised this when my daughter was born I asked my husband if he would move back to Europe so we were closer to family. He is American, but originally Turkish so we are closer to his family in Turkey too. My mother has been instrumental in helping me look after the kids and guiding me in this new endeavour of being a mum. I've never needed my own mother so much since becoming a mother myself - I realise how incredibly lucky I am to have her.

The baby months 0- 6 months

The baby months are much easier to manage without help or care as babies sleep for long (sometimes 20 hours) of periods of time, I found as long as I was working from home I could do most of my emailing and calls from my home office.

Nannies - best for 4-8 months

Nannies are great but expensive, this is usually someone who is a full trained childcare professional who know how to make the right food etc for baby. Because they are trained they will require a full-time salary.

Au Pairs - best for 6 months +

AuPairs are a fantastic option for great childcare and much cheaper than a nanny, that's because they are not a trained childcare professional so you do have to keep more on an eye on them and guide them and set expectations.

They are usually a young girl (sometimes boy) who is coming to learn English and your culture, they normally stay for between 4-6 months and they become a part of your family.

You need to invest some time into taking them on weekend trips and showing them around because it's a cultural exchange not just childcare.

Nursery

Both my children started nursery at around 8-9 months, I find at this age, they are getting inquisitive about their environment and need more stimuli than what's at home, some people say that's too early but

I find the nursery can offer them way more sensory experiences than I could ever offer on my own.

The psychological impact on children of being in care?

Sometimes I worry that my children have been in/are in care too much and what damage I am doing to them.

I have done some research on this, obviously a young child wants to be with their parents as much as possible, but as long as when you are with them, you show them undivided love and attention where they know you are a solid constant for them, then I think it's ok.

There are also huge benefits of children being in care like learning new skills; my son came back from nursery at 8 months old being able to use a spoon and my daughter still loves singing songs the Au Pair taught her.

Find a partner who helps

When we first landed in the UK after moving from the USA my husband didn't find a job for a very long time, so he helped me build our digital marketing business but I was doing all the sales, travelling into London for work and he was doing so much of the childcare.

He really has done a lot of the childcare over the years when I have been travelling for work and this has been key in giving me the freedom to attend important meetings and travel for work.

Build a support network

It's taken me 3.5 years to build, but now I have a support network of really great local women in my town who I can call on to look after the children, mainly women who work at my daughter's school or at my son's nursery (these women are great because I know they are from a trusted place)

Ask at your local nursery if any of the girls (yes it's mainly girls) do evening and weekend babysitting).

Work childcare costs into your billing.

This is something that I have only recently started doing, but sitting down and working out all your childcare costs on a spreadsheet and adding them to your business expenses because this is a cost that makes you available to work, so don't feel bad about working into your costs.

An introduction to the other startup mums:

1. Jesse Draper - Founding partner of Halogen Ventures (Raised $10million fund), mum of 2

2. Maggie Bolger, Founder Maggie & Rose (£35 million valuation), mum of 4.

3. Rachel Carrell, Founder Koru Kids,

(Raised £3.5 million while pregnant), mum of 2.

4. Andrea Sommer, Hiver.

(Www.hivertech.com) (Valuation £1.5million) mum of 3-month- old.

5. Lorraine Dallmeier, Director Formula Botanica (over £4.5 million in sales), mum of 2.

6. Sarah Kathleen Peck, founder Startup Pregnant, mum of 2.

Jesse Draper - Founding partner of Halogen Ventures ($10million fund), mum of 2.

Jesse Draper is founding partner of Halogen Ventures as well as creator and host of 2015 Emmy nominated television series,"The Valley Girl Show". Draper is a 4th generation venture capitalist focused on early stage investing in female founded consumer technology. Her portfolio includes Laurel & Wolf, Carbon38, Naya Health, HopSkipDrive, The Flex Company & Sugarfina. Through her show she's helped pioneer the way in digital media and has an initiative to interview 50% women in technology. Previously a Nickelodeon star, Draper has used her comedic talents to bring an approachable feel to the technology world, has produced and distributed over 300 interviews with some of the greatest minds in technology and beyond (including; Ted Turner, Mark Cuban, Sheryl Sandberg, Supreme Court Justice Sandra Day O'Connor, Jessica Alba, MC Hammer and Eric Schmidt) and was listed by Marie Claire magazine as one of the '50 Most Connected Women in America'. USA Today called the show "Must see startup TV". Draper is a contributor to Marie Claire, SV Magazine,

Mashable, Forbes.com, and is a regular investor and tech personality on shows including 'The Katie Couric Show', Fox's 'Good Day LA', CNBC's 'Who Wants to Be the Next Millionaire Inventor?' & Freeform'sStartup U. She proudly sits on the board of directors of Werk, the advisory board of Bizworld and is on the Chairman's board of SurfAir. Draper supports the Parkinson's Institute and is very involved with growing UCLA's female entrepreneurship community. She is a new mom, a graduate of UCLA and a Kappa Kappa Gamma.

Where were you at in your career when you decided to have kids?

I was at a real crossroads! Let me paint the picture. I was newly married. 29. I was in the final season of producing and hosting my Emmy nominated technology talk show The Valley Girl Show that I had built over the last 8 years of my life. I was pregnant, but I hadn't shared this with anyone yet and I was still the showrunner, also known as, I was heading up EVERYTHING. I was writing, producing, booking, hosting and if you have ever been in production with a skeleton crew, you know I was doing everything including taking out the trash.

We had hired an external production company that shall remain nameless and were in the final week of the show. They were young, stupid, and weird things had begun happening with their team. We paid on time, by episode and only after the final product was delivered (as I recommend doing with any 'wild west' or frankly consulting profession). Towards the end of filming, I walk into the editing bay, one newer person on the team tells me, Mike has taken the hard drives and said you have to pay him. Mike was our outsourced producer. As I had paid him the day before for the delivered footage, I was confused. Upon calling producer 'Mike', he basically told me that he was 'blackmailing' me for $25,000 and holding the hard drives hostage. We had been paying on time, this was not in the budget. I was confused. He was nuts. He said, 'Meet me at 8PM in a particular parking lot with a check for $25,000," And only then, he would give me the hard drives. Here is the predicament besides the technology hard drive hostages: if I could get the hard drives back, I still only had 48 hours to edit and deliver the footage to San Francisco. In addition, I also had to find and train a new local editor because this guy, and his company, was clearly fired. I called my lawyer, I called my Dad, both said, 'DO NOT GO MEET SOME GUY IN A PARKING LOT!' What did I do? I met him at 8PM in a random parking lot in LA. I rolled down the window 1 inch and then 5 inched when i realized the hard drives couldn't get through. I refused to get out of the car. He ultimately gave me all the hard drives and then I gave him a check. I then asked him 'What are you thinking? Is this how you do business? We have been working together for weeks?' I scolded him and I made him cry tears - a very confusing outcome. I put a stop payment on the check.

I could say that after 8 years of both good and bad producers, casting couch moments, crazy independent production companies that blackmail people in the industry, this was the moment that I decided I was leaving the media industry but actually that wasn't it. I stayed up for 48 hours straight. I trained a new editor starting at midnight that night. Some young guy who just rolled with it and I provided a whole lot of Red Bull and caffeine oriented beverages. Again, I was newly pregnant and also getting sick every couple of hours as it was my first trimester. I could literally only eat bagels. Around 6AM the morning after this, I had been up all night with this new editor. I ran out to Noah's bagels. I'm in pajamas, I look like crap. No one is in Noah's bagels except for.....Conan O'Brien. The talk show host. I cannot tell you, for the life of me, how many talk show hosts I tried to grab a meeting with for advice on running a talk show. I couldn't sit down with any of them. Here I was, 8 years in and Conan O'Brien is just sitting in my local Noah's bagels at 6AM on a Tuesday reading his email on his phone. I ordered my 3 bagels and I went up to him. I told him I was a fan, I told him about the issues I was having at my show and he said, you will always be pushing a rock up a mountain, just keep going. We talked for about 20 minutes and he truly couldn't have been nicer. I ran back to meet my editor and told him that Conan said it was all going to be ok!

We powered through and completed the last episode of the season and delivered it to the network. I came home, still in pajamas. My husband looked at me and said 'You are pregnant. This is not humanly sustainable.' Simultaneously, I had made an initiative to interview 50% women in technology on the show. This was in 2009, so harder to find women in technology. Finally, women came! They pitched me and sometimes I would tell them, "Your company is too early for the show, but I love what you are doing. Maybe I can write you a tiny check and be a strategic investor/advisor.' These early investments included companies like Eloquii and This is L. both of which have now sold for $100 Million. My husband pointed out that in addition to not sleeping and running the show, I was also running a small venture fund. I had never realized I would have to choose, I thought I could run a talk show full time and also run the VC fund. However, I had NO idea what was coming when you throw kids into the mix. I'm not saying you can't do it all, but I now say that the talk show is on hiatus indefinitely. That is where I was in my career when I decided to have kids.

What has been key in being able to have children and grow your businesses at the same time? (please give practical advice!)

Ask for help from friends, figure out a childcare schedule. I now have 2 kids. I am incredibly lucky. I have a nanny and I have an assistant at work. I couldn't survive without them. They are the reason I can 'do it all'. Sometimes I have my team work from my house. One of the verticals we want to invest in with this current fund is childcare because in the United States, it is really broken for families with 2 working parents. It is unaffordable, parents work until 6 and kids are in school until 2 or 3 so you still need to pay for childcare.

Divide and Conquer: I also have a husband who I call a 50/50 co-parent. He is truly the man of my dreams. We have to divide and conquer. We try our best to make sure one of us is always home as we both travel quite a bit for work. We used to have so many silly fights about who was doing more. Now we just decide who is doing the dishes, laundry, organising playdates and when the handyman is coming and put one person in charge.While we both try to be involved, we only have one of us go to parent teacher conferences or events at school as one of us is usually in a meeting. We have google calendars for work and we bought a large laminated white board calendar for the kids schedules that we have up in our kitchen.

Time with kids: I wake up early and cook breakfast for the kids from 6-7:30 every morning and I feel like that is some special time I get with them during my day.

Taking care of your well being:This is an important thing that Mom's typically don't do. Let me tell you, I didn't take care of myself and ended up in the hospital last summer so this is important. Hydrate. Exercise. Do something for you. The things I am missing in my life that I haven't mastered is maintaining a social life and working out regularly. I have really had to think about what is important when it comes to taking time away from the kids as you can't spend time with everyone. I have learned to say 'No' more easily to nighttime work events and some weekend activities. I want to be with my kids in my free time. I'm at a point in my family/work life where I have realized there is a shift. I have some friends who are upset about me not spending enough time with them and I have some who understand because they are having kids as well. My husband and I just prioritise our family lives regularly.

And for work, I always tell my assistant that my calendar is fluid. I have somewhere between 20-30 meetings/calls a week. I have made some ground rules when it comes to my schedule. Calls can always be rescheduled. Meetings I try my best to stick to or move 48 hours in advance. Every week, I go through my calendar and decide what my priorities are and then reschedule the Friday before accordingly. I have started to just say no to any work conferences on the weekend. I am not even sure why people still throw those. I have also begun blocking out my Friday afternoons from 3-6PM for walk/hike meetings. I realised it's a great way to ease into the weekend and do something for myself as opposed to monotonous meeting after meeting.

What have been some of the hardest moments? (please be as real and honest as possible)

The days our nanny cancels at the last minute are the worst. It happens. My nanny once cancelled and I had a really important pitch for my first fund. I didn't want to reschedule and I told her, 'I don't want to reschedule our meeting today but my nanny just cancelled.' She said 'I'm 8 months pregnant and I'll come to your house.' I gave her a full powerpoint pitch with my 2 year old running around screaming in the corner and I closed her. I am forever grateful for that meeting.

Take care of yourself. Last year, I had a new baby, moved, my husband switched jobs, my grandmother passed away and it was a very trying time on our family. This was already a full load, keep in mind, I also couldn't take time off when I had the baby as I am the CEO of my fund. Because I hadn't been taking care of myself, one weekend, I had both kids with me and my husband was away for work, my body broke down. In 24 hours, I broke a finger, tore my calf muscle in 2 and was rushed to hospital for dehydration. 3 separate ailments. I then left the hospital on crutches (by the way, with a new baby, a knee scooter is a much better option). This was a great wakeup call for me. I couldn't just work and take care of everyone. I needed to carve out time for myself. An hour here or there. And even splurging on some babysitting time on the weekend helps your sanity. We try not to do it often but it is definitely worth it when you are burnt out.

2. Maggie Bolger, Founder Maggie & Rose (£25 million valuation), mum of 4.

Maggie & Rose was the first Private Family Members Club in the UK – a unique concept born with the aim to create an inviting space for families to play and create. Maggie & Rose cultivates creativity in children through art and play whilst providing a community for parents to meet, seek, share and escape, in a safe, home from home environment.

Maggie & Rose has become a brand in its own right focusing primarily on supporting the early stages of education, providing Cooking, Art, Music, Drama and Dance classes for pre-schoolers. The classes are carefully adapted so little ones from just three months old can join in, these classes are extended and developed to meet the needs of older children during holiday periods.

Where were you at in your career when you decided to have kids?

I didn't have a career! I had my first child at 22, whilst on an extend gap years from Uni, still trying to figure out what I wanted to do when I grew up. Having been a member of Soho House, and feeling particularly isolated and lonely once i had my kids, I realised the gaping hole in the market I was living and breathing, so with 3 kids in tow, I went about setting up cool club for parents to meet, have great coffee, do relatively inspiring activities in a place that was designed for us as much as the kids.

What has been key in being able to have children and grow your businesses at the same time? (please give practical advice!)

Getting good help where you can, a good cleaner, trustworthy babysitter that you can call on, friends that are happy to do the odd after school pick up - building up that network of people you can call on to help when the shit hits that fan - or you just need a night off!

Total support from family, so the most critical, being close enough so they can jump in when needed.

My mum moved over from NZ and looked after the kids and the home for me, without this sacrifice on her part, I wouldn't have been able to do what i did. For which i will be eternally grateful. It is a common part of Indian culture for grandparents to do this,

She allowed me to be in startup mode, crazy hours, most of the time i had no idea what i was doing and was having to learn so much, whilst also having to be up and night and deal with things like Chicken pox and the likes. I was lucky that the kids were a part of the business so they were always around hanging out and taking part in the classes. They were my human guinea pigs as we tested everything on them.

What have been some of the hardest moments? (please be as real and honest as possible)

Trying to be wife, mother and boss, juggling all of these things and putting pressure on myself to be everything to everyone never works and it broke me.

My marriage ended because of this, I had been way too stressed to be present and engage with the kids as much as i should have. Made no effort to be a wife, forgot about that relationship and let the distance grow because i was too busy with the business. I think because I have so many kids and my mum was there, it allowed me to be more distant that i should have been, as they had each other and were a real tribe.

So being present is a big one - and one of the toughest, being able to compartmentalise work from home, and shut it off. I still struggle with this and I probably always will. The end of my marriage forced me to deal with this, a tough lesson to learn, but now I try to be more present for the kids. Banning the phones and computers and having family meals together are just small things that i try and do so we have some quality time together.

3. Rachel Carrell, Founder Koru Kids, (Raised £3.5 million while pregnant), mum of 2.

Koru Kids (www.korukids.co.uk) is on a mission to improve childcare in London. We train and provide after school nannies, and arrange nanny shares. Sharing nannies means that a single nanny looks after children from 2 families at once. Each family pays less, the nanny gets paid more, and the children get a friend to play with.

Innovation in childcare is desperately needed. Did you know that most families with children spend as much on childcare as they do on their mortgage? Or that the average cost of a full time nanny in Central London is £37,000? (Remember, that comes out of your post-tax income). Did you know that nurseries aren't much cheaper than that, if you have two children? Did you know that many nurseries shut for summer holidays, or only do half days, and that if your child is sick they can't go for the next 48 hours? Did you know that if you get a nanny, you have to run a PAYE scheme for her and - from next year - also a pension scheme, with a completely different regulator?

If you're a parent, you probably knew all of that, plus much more about the pain of sorting out your childcare.

Koru Kids was founded to solve these problems. The mission brings together several things I care deeply about: the critical importance of positive early childhood experiences; the need for real choices for women in the workplace; and the potential of great tech to solve market failures.

Where were you at in your career when you decided to have kids?

I was quite bored toward the end of my long years working in a big corporate and very ready to have kids -- but I didn't have a husband, and for me that was an important prerequisite. Unfortunately by the time I solved that problem, I was CEO of a startup which was much more interesting and also harder to combine with having kids. I had my first one in that job, and my second one as CEO of a different startup. The one saving grace was that the startups didn't involve any travel at all, which made the whole thing more manageable. Having kids at the corporate would have involved a much more generous maternity leave but once I'd gone back to work, the international travel involved would have been really hard.

What has been key in being able to have children and grow your businesses at the same time? (please give practical advice!)

I would say this, because I run a childcare tech startup, but: having the right support around you is utterly invaluable. I believe being a working parent is the 'crunch time' of your whole life. You are a child, then a student, then a young working person, then a working parent with young kids, then your kids get older and leave home, and then you retire.

Of all those stages, the most exhausting, stressful, pressured stage is the one when you are trying to work and also bring up small children.

This is the time to dip into your savings, if you are lucky enough to have any, the time to pay people to help you, pay for good quality ready meals, call in favours you built up in your 20s, say 'yes please' whenever anyone offers to help out. You cannot do it all alone.

I am also a strong believer in the power of low standards for housework. Spend time with your kids, run a great business, have a gleaming home: pick any two. I'd rather

be playing a board game with my daughter than tidying up the toys. So our house is pretty messy.

What have been some of the hardest moments? (please be as real and honest as possible)

My baby is not a very good sleeper.

Sometimes I am bent over his cot stroking his back for hours in the evening, knowing how much work I still have to do once he's finally asleep. Weekends are not relaxing like they are for my childfree team members.

They're exhausting. My 'me time' is sitting quietly reading emails. It's hard to find time for a haircut and I haven't read a novel in about three years.

I raised my last round while pregnant - I had a baby in the middle of the fundraise - and in general it was quite a positive experience, although also the hardest thing I'd ever done.

A few days after the birth when I went into the office for the day, I started bleeding really heavily all of a sudden. It was terrifying, I thought I was dying.

I called the midwife and she was quite calm, saying this was common especially among mums who had older children and were running after them, doing too much too soon after the birth.

In my case I was running after my business, but it came to the same thing medically speaking.

Every mum has hard moments --

it's just that the mixture is a little different when you're combining a business and motherhood.

4. Andrea Sommer, Hiver. (Www.hivertech.com) (Valuation £1.5million) mum of 3 month old.

Andrea Sommer is the founder & CEO of Hiver. Hiver is a female-founded, majority women technology company that helps event marketers measure and improve engagement at their events by enabling networkers to remember the names of every contact they meet and to quickly connect with those they find valuable. It is designed to connect in-person with the digital networking experience.

Andrea is passionate about technology, entrepreneurship, increasing the number of women represented in both, from entry-level to board-level. She has spoken at numerous conferences on technology, the mobile industry, entrepreneurship, raising start-up finance, investing, being a female founder and women in technology.

Previously, Andrea was Director of Strategic Initiatives Europe at Avanade, a joint venture between Accenture & Microsoft. She also consulted for other technology brands including Microsoft in the US, South America and Europe.

Andrea has been featured in press publications such as The Financial Times, Forbes, Medium and Thrive Global as well as in the book The MBA Entrepreneur. Hiver has also been featured in The New York Times.

She is the co-host of the London Female Founders Breakfast series, bringing together female founders to share, learn, and support each other through the journey of entrepreneurship.

She holds a Bachelor's Degree from Reed College in Portland, US and an Executive MBA from London Business School.

Where were you at in your career when you decided to have kids?

I left it quite late to have a baby as I am now 39 and had my daughter when I was 38.

For a really long time the idea of having children seemed to be incompatible with my life, both before I was an entrepreneur and after.

When I was about to turn 38, I was cooking dinner one night with my husband and I was overcome with this great sadness. I looked at him, and the relationship we'd built over 17 years and it made me heartbroken to think that this would be it, that he'd be the end of his line.

Until then I had never really felt like I wanted children but at that moment it really changed for me.

That same night I told him what I was thinking and he said he'd be ok with us trying. Thankfully I got pregnant right away despite my age.

What has been key in being able to have children and grow your businesses at the same time? (please give practical advice!)

The main thing is flexibility - both in terms of how you structure your work and your personal life.

I am lucky that Hiver is already a fully flexible organisation - our team is fully remote.

We are used to working across different timezones and using video conferencing to get things done.

We are used to seeing each other on camera uncensored - cats, dogs, kids, family and other guest appearances are frequent.

Flexibility also matters externally. There is no reason why you can't attend a coffee with an investor and have your baby with you, or bring the baby to pitch events.

Just last week I did exactly that - I brought the baby with me to an investor meeting.

The investor was thrilled to see her and spent most of the meeting holding the baby.

I'm not saying it is right for every situation but there are many situations where we have the urge to hide the baby but in reality the two lives can co-exist.

Last month I had signed up for a pitch event as part of my fundraising efforts and I asked the organisation whether I could bring the baby along.

One of my colleagues had offered to look after her while I was pitching, since she'd only be 7 weeks old by that point and I didn't want to be away from her for the six or more hours it would have taken to get to the event, pitch, network and return home. The organisation was flexible with the practice session and allowed me to dial in to present.

Sadly for the pitch day they felt they could not accommodate the baby - so I ended up leaving her at home with her dad which was quite tough.

More flexibility is needed here too - supporting women entrepreneurs requires supporting mothers and that includes childcare. It was a missed opportunity for them to really go above and beyond to support the female entrepreneurs they claim to want to support.

Getting fathers more involved is also key. My husband changed roles a couple of months before the baby arrived to a role where he wasn't travelling as much so he could really co-parent. Now we split our days so that he looks after the baby in the morning, until about midday while I work, go to yoga or run errands.

Then he works from 12 until the evening while I look after the baby. He mostly works from home so if I have a call or something urgent to deal with he is right there to look after the baby.

This approach is working really well for us now while I'm not fully back at work. Once I return my plan is to have a nanny who will flex around my schedule and enable me to continue going to baby activities and breast feeding while supporting me in doing work that cannot be flexed (some client meetings for instance).

What have been some of the hardest moments? (please be as real and honest as possible)

I'm pretty new to being a parent but one moment come to mind. This was when I told my board that I was pregnant. That meeting was absolutely terrible. I got some very negative comments about my pregnancy and impending motherhood including:

That I had broken an unspoken contract between myself and my investors by getting pregnant.

That when one of the board members was running and growing her business she chose to not have children, and that as a result she was really successful in that venture and now has a really nice house.

That investors are probably wondering why I chose to get pregnant when I did.

That she found it 'hard to believe' that investors would put additional money into the business knowing that I was pregnant.

Obviously these comments were really shocking and upsetting. I responded with a note expressing my displeasure and also using this as an opportunity to educate them on the many examples of women who successfully balance motherhood with business / politics / etc.

It was a really painful experience for me and it permanently damaged the trusted relationship I had built with them. I am not certain we have recovered yet - and in this round I am not feeling as supported and I have in the past.

5 . Lorraine Dallmeier, Director of Formula Botanica (over £4.5m in sales), Mum of 2.

Lorraine Dallmeier runs Formula Botanica, the award-winning online Organic Cosmetic Science School, which has trained more than 6,000 organic skincare entrepreneurs to start or grow their own indie beauty brand in 140+ countries around the world.

Formula Botanica has seen hundreds of its graduates launch successful indie beauty brands, many of which are now stocked by retailers all over the world, have won awards and have picked up rave reviews from customers.

Lorraine took over Formula Botanica when it was its infancy, taking it from a £20,000 a year turnover to the multi-million pound business it is today. She concluded the purchase with a toddler by her side, a baby on her hip and a team of lawyers. Lorraine then found herself juggling motherhood and business, having two children under the age of 4, and a start-up to look after by herself. In the last five years, she has grown the business from a one-woman website to a global organisation with a team of professionals.

Along with being a teaching institution, Formula Botanica is also a publishing company and attracts 100,000+ readers per month to its info-packed blog where the School tackles topics on organic formulation and beauty entrepreneurship, as well as publishing the popular Green Beauty Conversations podcast, which hit the #1 spot in the Fashion & Beauty category in iTunes within its first 24 hours of launching.

Lorraine won the Digital Achiever of the Year award at the 2018 CEW Achiever Awards, judged by Google. She also led Formula Botanica to win the 2016 gold award for 'Excellence in the Design of Learning Content' at the international Learning Technologies Awards.

Prior to growing Formula Botanica to a multi-million pound teaching institution, Lorraine worked and lived in the UK, Netherlands, USA, Russia and Australia. Lorraine is a Chartered Environmentalist (CEnv), full member of the Royal Society of Biology (RSB), full member of the Society of Cosmetic Scientists (SCS) and

A full Member of the Institute of
Environmental Management &
Assessment.

She has been voted into the top
influencers list in the natural beauty
industry for four consecutive years.

Where were you at in your career when you decided to have kids?

I had been working on my career as an environmental scientist in the international energy sector for a decade. I was managing large-scale infrastructure developments with a team of people reporting to me. My job was well paid, I was well looked after and I was receiving weekly calls from headhunters because the industry was booming. I was 30 and it seemed like a good time to have kids.

My partner was very keen to start a family and we were thrilled when I found out I was pregnant with our first son. I took my full maternity leave, staggered back to work after a year, still severely sleep deprived, and resumed my job, this time taking on even more responsibility. A year later, I got pregnant again.

Cue my next maternity leave and then ... crickets. I returned to work after having had our second son and it was as if I was invisible. All those years of experience, all those letters to my name, all those millions I'd made for my employers - it had all been relegated to the history books by me disappearing for a year to have our child. I got put in the attic at work and had nothing to do.

Luckily I had long seen the writing on the wall and had started to work on my own business soon after the birth of our first son. In fact, during my second maternity leave I had also bought a small start-up company with my savings, with the intention of building a side hustle. What I didn't realise at the time, was that my side hustle would become my million pound business within 3 short years.

What has been key in being able to have children and grow your businesses at the same time? (please give practical advice!)

I run my business from home, which meant that I could just about stay afloat juggling looking after my children and my company. I breastfed my kids for a combined total of 5.5 years and I wanted to be there for them as they're only little for such a short time. Unfortunately we don't have family nearby, so we really were flying solo on this one.

A few things were key in being able to grow my children and my business:
Smart phones. It is simply amazing how much you can get done on a phone while your children feed and sleep on you.

My two were ferocious breastfeeders and terrible sleepers, so would generally only nap when they were either on me or in the car. For that reason, I conducted a lot of work for my online business with a mobile - with my kids asleep on me... or in the car. My partner. He also works from home and could help when things got desperate. When the kids and business were young, he was still travelling for work and frequently up against major client deadlines, but at least he was there when I needed him the most.

Now we've managed to retire him from work for good, thanks to the growth of my business, so I have a lot more support. Nighttime work.

I wanted my business to succeed so badly and was prepared to work myself to the bone to make it happen, because I could see the potential for it supporting my whole family.

When my children slept (which didn't happen much!), I worked. It didn't matter how tired I was, I just kept going because I kept my eyes on the end goal.

Childcare: My kids went to a childminder two days a week as it was good for them and good for me. It got them socialising with other kids and it gave me a window to work.

Hiring people to help: As my business grew, so did my ability to hire people. I started taking on contractors to help take on parts of the business, such as customer service and IT. Some of those initial contractors are now employees and still work with me, years later.

Mum groups: Going out of the house and socialising with other mums locally kept me sane and helped me focus on what was important.

Although working from home isn't always easy, I'm proud to say that my business model has also attracted in other working mothers to my team, who have helped make Formula Botanica the success it is today.

The flexibility afforded by home working arrangements allows women to have a job and a family at the same time and, in my opinion, is the future for forward-thinking companies.

What have been some of the hardest moments? (please be as real and honest as possible)

The toughest and lowest point for me was the day a tractor sliced through our internet cables, exactly half an hour after I'd gone live with the online course launch I'd been preparing for a month.

My partner was away for work, our internet provider Plusnet refused to talk to me because his name was the only one listed on our account, and I had a demanding toddler and a constantly feeding baby at home with me, so I couldn't go and work in an Internet cafe instead.

This is the only moment that has reduced me to tears in my business.

The entire village ended up in an Internet blackout for 3 days. 4G hadn't arrived yet so I had no mobile options either.

However, by some complete fluke, our neighbours directly opposite were the only people in the entire village who hadn't been cut off.

They very kindly let me use their WiFi password, which would only work when I propped open the letterbox and sat on the bottom stair with my laptop.

So that's how I simultaneously ran my launch and looked after the kids for three days. I sold £65k of online courses that week, sat on the bottom stair next to an open letterbox and running after the children.

The second worst thing has been the enormous amount of colds, bugs and even parasites (!) my kids have brought home from nursery and school over the years.

Because I was so sleep deprived for years (we didn't sleep properly for 6 years after the kids were born) and because I was working so hard, I was very run down and susceptible to any bug they threw at me.

When you work for yourself, you're far less likely to take a day off sick so I've just kept going through every ailment. I have coughed uncontrollably through many a live webinar, stood in front of cameras when I could barely keep going and once even had to host a 3-day live conference for 100 people after a week of gastroenteritis, courtesy of my youngest son.

I didn't eat for most of those three days on stage and am still not entirely sure how I got through it. It's only now that my kids are at school that I'm starting to find their immune system is becoming more robust and we're getting fewer colds, which has certainly made my working life a lot easier!

6. Sarah Kathleen Peck

Sarah Peck is a writer, startup advisor, and yoga teacher based in New York City. She's the founder and executive director of Startup Pregnant, a media company documenting the stories of women's leadership across work and family. She hosts the weekly Startup Pregnant podcast, a show about working parents, entrepreneurs, and motherhood.

Previously, she worked at Y Combinator backed One Month, Inc, a company that teaches people to code in 30 days, and prior, as a writing and communications consultant.

She's a 20-time All-American swimmer who successfully swam the Escape from Alcatraz nine separate times, once wearing only a swim cap and goggles to raise $33k for charity: water. To date, she's written for more than 75 different web publications and and has delivered speeches and workshops at Penn, UVA, Berkeley, Harvard, Year of the X, Craft & Commerce, WDS, and more.

One recent viral essay, *The Art of Asking*, has been used across tech companies and product teams to train teams in clear communications.

She's currently writing a memoir of her experience working in the tech startup world while she was pregnant with her first kid.

Where were you at in your career when you decided to have kids?

In 2015, I was thirty and just married, and I was 9 months into working at a startup in New York City. I was the communications director, and then VP of Product, for an online education company focused on teaching people how to code. We taught coding skills in simple, easy-to-follow videos that were short and fast, and people built their new tech projects right away (within a month or less).

We were too small of a team for us to have any benefits from the government for parental leave, paid or unpaid, so I had to negotiate with the founders in order to take time away to have children.

I had my first kid within two years of working at the company, and then I left to start writing a book shortly thereafter. The book surprised me, because I was so focused on writing that I didn't see myself setting up for a new business before it almost hit me over the head.

I was writing a book, and I started a podcast so I could interview women entrepreneurs to be a part of the book.

I got sponsors for the podcast right away, and launched a mastermind program for my audience, and suddenly I was creating products and services that people were paying for, and not only was I writing a book; I was running my own company.

My second kid was born recently, about three years into the journey of growing my business and writing my book.

I'm currently running a company as a solo-preneur with two kids under three (both in full-time daycare), and with four contractors that help me as well.

What has been key in being able to have children and grow your businesses at the same time? (please give practical advice!)

This is a complicated question, and a challenging one, because I think the social structures in my country (the United States) need to be far better to support parents and families.

We're about to hit a huge caretaking crisis (something I've written about for Forbes), and Harvard Business Review just released a new report showing how much companies are going to be affected by the needs of employees who have family members, from young kids to aging parents, that require the help of caretakers. So before I can give individual or company-level tips, I'd have to say one of the biggest things is having a country that supports parents and early childhood, paid parental leave available for all parents, regardless of employment status, and community support for working parents (moms and dads alike).

With those pieces in place, one of the biggest keys for me has been having a relationship with my partner where we articulate, in detail, our dreams and goals for the future.

We aspire to the highest levels of freedom and creativity, and we both want to create work that matters in the world.

To do so, we've created a shared goal of spending far less than we make, and being able to live off of one person's salary at any given time, so that we can spend our shared energy pursuing projects and work that matters. I used my savings and the ability to lean on my partner's employment to dig in and launch the book and the business, something that most entrepreneurs need—research by the Kaufmann foundation shows that most entrepreneurs usually need about $25k-$30k to get off the ground, and that this financial bolster often looks like: the ability to live rent-free in a parent's home; borrowing assets or utilities to get the initial push; or another form of gift or loan that makes the venture possible.

If both of these things are in place (social infrastructure, an injection of cash or access to assets), then entrepreneurship becomes tenable and do-able.

For me, having access to high-quality, reliable childcare to the tune of 40 hours per week (sometimes 45) has been key.

I am not one of those people that can work and do baby things at the same time. I also require sane amounts of sleep.

Many of the things I choose to do are boring: I go to bed around 9PM and skip evening events because they are too disruptive to my workdays and my brain functioning.

I exercise daily to keep my anxiety in check. I ask for a ton of help and when people offer help, I try to almost always say yes.

I remember that building things is slow and can take a long time, and try to stay in touch with people who keep me grounded and motivated so that I can keep going.

What have been some of the hardest moments? (please be as real and honest as possible)

The business I'm working on, Startup Pregnant, is a place to support women entrepreneurs who are navigating work and pregnancy, and early parenthood, and trying to figure out how to take leave, build sustainable businesses, develop resilient systems and infrastructure for long-term success, and create businesses that support them and their life dreams.

There is a tide shift happening right now where people are starting to pay attention to, and highlight, the lives of working parents. It's incredible—from the New York Times' Parenting section, to the WIRED families and Facebook groups, to the Atlantic articles on family life. It seems like every day there's a new initiative for working parents, and it reflects a lot of what is changing in our society every day.

At the same time, it's remarkable hard to create 100 episodes of a podcast, to write for years at a time, and devote yourself to a cause and wake up to see that an entire newspaper has done what you've done and it reaches a huge audience. There are days when I have been so demoralised by how hard I'm working that it takes me scraping the bottom to keep going.

Being an independent entrepreneur is one of the hardest things I've ever done, and being a parent is also one of the hardest things I've ever done—and I've had major surgery for a blood clot, had a rib removed from my body, swam the Escape From Alcatraz, and was a college swimmer.

There's a lot I've done with my life, and parenting and entrepreneurship will challenge every belief you have about who you are and what you're capable of doing. It took a few nights for me to sleep, to cry, and to re-set, and to dig back in and keep going.

The overall news is positive: that so many people are interested in this means we can collectively work to change the culture, to grow, to make things happen far faster. I continue to edit and refine and recalibrate. I think that one of the biggest myths of entrepreneurship is that you can come up with an idea, build it, and sell it. In my experience, and in what I've learned through research and listening, the true grit comes from editing your idea, and editing again, and refining, and changing, and listening to thousands of customers, and being willing to continue to shift and change to meet the market to truly solve a problem in a way that people are willing to spend money on, fast enough before you run out of time, money, or stamina. It's hard.

I believe that we pursue projects and goals not because of the outcome or the way that we think ticking some achievement off a list will make us feel, but because of the way the pursuit of the goal changes how we show up in the world.

Goals are attractive because they indicate to us a greater sense of self capability: we want to be people who write every day, or who can show up every day to build a company, or who lift weights and exercise daily.

Entrepreneurship has asked me to show up every day and discover where the weak spots are in my mind, to uncover the hidden stories of my own psychology, and to grapple with my Self in a way that makes me feel like I may break, daily. It reminds me of the tough work I did in college to become an athlete: every day I pushed myself to the limit and wondered whether or not I would ever be capable of what I hoped. Some days I was more capable, and I could look at myself with astonishment. Some days I failed a dozen times, and then a dozen times again, and I quietly ate brownies, tears in my eyes, before calling it a night and trying again the next day.

Parenting is very similar. I see it as an opportunity to study the stories of my family, and to make a conscious choice about what I want to bring to my children, while simultaneously letting go of any attachment to the outcome, knowing that these children are their own beings and will likely do things very differently than me.

I joke with them that they will get to go to therapy to undo all the things that I have taught them, and to reconcile with who they are—and that it's okay for this to happen. Parenting is also an excruciating kind of boredom, at times: the relentlessness of it has not been well captured by our myths of what motherhood looks like.

Is there anything more mundane than changing your thousandth diaper? Being peed on is cute until you're trying to get out the door to an employee meeting and your shirt is now stinky, sticky, and wet. But it's dealing with all of this minutiae that also shows us who we really are—not in the grand, sweeping, idealistic moments but in the actual patterns of everyday life.

My two cents? Develop resilience, and keep developing it. Find ways to strengthen your inner resolve, and ways to stay motivated. Taking care of yourself is imperative, because it is through your friendship calls, and your parenting meet-up groups, and your CEO masterminds that you will laugh-cry through a bottle of wine, or shake off the struggles, or figure out how to fire the person you have to let go of.

www.ingramcontent.com/pod-product-compliance
Lightning Source LLC
Chambersburg PA
CBHW060638210326
41520CB00010B/1651